TOP TEN
BIGGEST

Ben Hubbard

The Great Pyramid, Egypt

Publisher: Melissa Fairley
Art Director: Faith Booker
Editor: Emma Dods
Designer: Emma Randall
Production Controller: Ed Green
Production Manager: Suzy Kelly

ISBN: 978 1 84898 211 6

Copyright © TickTock Entertainment Ltd. 2010
First published in Great Britain in 2010 by TickTock Entertainment Ltd.,
The Old Sawmill, 103 Goods Station Road, Tunbridge Wells, Kent, TN1 2DP

Printed in China
1 3 5 7 9 10 8 6 4 2

Picture credits (t=top; b=bottom; c=centre; l=left; r=right; OFC=outside front cover):
A & J Visage/Alamy: 21. Courtesy of Mallie's Sports Bar & Grill: 4, 6–7, 7b. Crystal Lagoons: 22–23. Danita
Dellmont/Alamy: 25. Jean-Paul Ferrero/ardea.com: 16. George Hall/Corbis: 12–13. Motoring Picture Library/Alamy: 18-19.
NASA Jet Propulsion Laboratory (NASA-JPL)/courtesy of nasaimages.com: 28–29. Renaud Visage/Getty Images: 20.
Dennis Scott/Corbis: OFC, 5b, 16–17. Shutterstock: 1, 2, 14–15, 24, 26, 27 both. Solent News/Rex Features: 5t, 10–11.

Thank you to Lorraine Petersen and the members of nasen

Every effort has been made to trace copyright holders, and we apologize in advance for any omissions.
We would be pleased to insert the appropriate acknowledgements in any subsequent edition of this publication.

NOTE TO READERS
The website addresses are correct at the time of publishing. However, due to the ever-changing
nature of the internet, websites and content may change. Some websites can contain links that
are unsuitable for children. The publisher is not responsible for changes in content or website
addresses. We advise that internet searches should be supervised by an adult.

*An African
bush elephant*

CONTENTS

INTRODUCTION

This book is all about the world's biggest things.

From **BIG** burgers...

...to **BIG** animals...

...to **BIG** machines...

This huge burger weighed 84.19 kilograms. The beef burger took 15 hours to cook!

The world's biggest motorbike is so huge that it can crush cars!

The blue whale is the world's biggest animal. Its tongue can weigh as much as an elephant!

BIGGEST BURGER

The biggest commercially available burger can be found at Mallie's Sports Grill & Bar, USA.

The beef burger alone needed three men to carry it. After 15 hours in the oven, it was then covered with bacon, cheese, lettuce, tomatoes, onion and pickle. After that it was put in a huge bun.

If you fancy trying one of these "Absolutely Ridiculous Burgers" you will need to order it three days in advance.

Start saving... each burger costs $499 (£316)!

BIGGEST FOOD FIGHT

On the last Wednesday of August, the biggest annual food fight takes place in Buñol, Spain.

Several lorries transport tomatoes into town – over 100,000 kilograms in total.

Tens of thousands of people from all over the world take part.

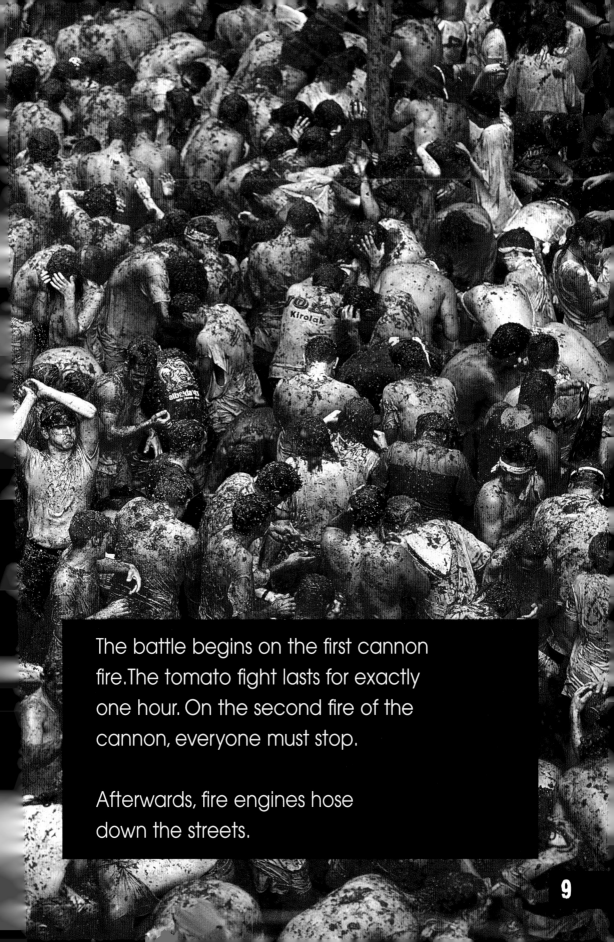

The battle begins on the first cannon fire.The tomato fight lasts for exactly one hour. On the second fire of the cannon, everyone must stop.

Afterwards, fire engines hose down the streets.

BIGGEST MOTORBIKE

It took retired stuntman Ray Baumann three years to build the "Monster Motorbike".

It is the biggest motorbike in the world. The bike is nine metres long and three metres high.

It also weighs 13,600 kilograms – that's about as heavy as a bus.

BIGGEST AIRCRAFT

The *Antonov An-225 Mriya* is the biggest aircraft ever.

Space shuttle

This is a specially built Russian cargo plane. It can "piggyback" big objects. Even other aircraft.

Here, it is carrying the "Buran" space shuttle on its back.

- Length: 84 metres
- Wingspan: 88.4 metres
- Top speed: 850 kilometres per hour
- Weight (when empty): 285,000 kilograms

BIGGEST LAND ANIMAL

The African bush elephant is the biggest animal on land.

Everything about this elephant
is **BIG!**

It can grow up to:
- 10 metres in length
- 4 metres in height (to the shoulder)
- 6,000 kilograms in weight.

Not surprisingly, African bush elephants have enormous appetites. They eat up to 136 kilograms of vegetation every day.

BIGGEST SEA ANIMAL

The blue whale is the biggest animal in the sea and also on the planet! It can weigh as much as 30 African bush elephants. Even its heart weighs as much as a small car!

Krill

The blue whale eats up to four tonnes of krill every day.

The blue whale can grow up to:
- Length: 30 metres
- Weight: 180,000 kilograms

BIGGEST PRODUCTION CAR

The Bugatti *Royale type 41* is the biggest production car in the world. The car has held this title since it was first built.

Manufactured between 1926 and 1933, only six cars were ever built!

- Length: 6.7 metres
- Weight: 3,250 kilograms

BIGGEST FLOWER

The biggest flower in the world is called *Rafflesia arnoldi.*

It is 91 centimetres across and can weigh up to 11 kilograms.

Oddly, this southeast Asian beauty smells like rotting meat! Luckily the flies that pollinate the plant love the smell.

Once it has fully developed, the flower only lives for a few days.

BIGGEST SWIMMING POOL

The biggest swimming pool in the world is a whopping 1,013 metres long.

Only an Olympic athlete could swim laps of the San Alfonso del Mar in Chile, South America.

Luckily, you can sail around it instead.

Six thousand normal swimming pools can fit inside it!

The pool covers eight hectares and holds
249 million litres of filtered seawater.

A computer sucks water in from the sea
at one end and pumps it out at the other.

BIGGEST TOMB

The Great Pyramid in Egypt is the biggest tomb on Earth.

It was constructed 4,500 years ago from 2.3 million limestone blocks.

Each block weighs between 2.3 and 13.6 tonnes!

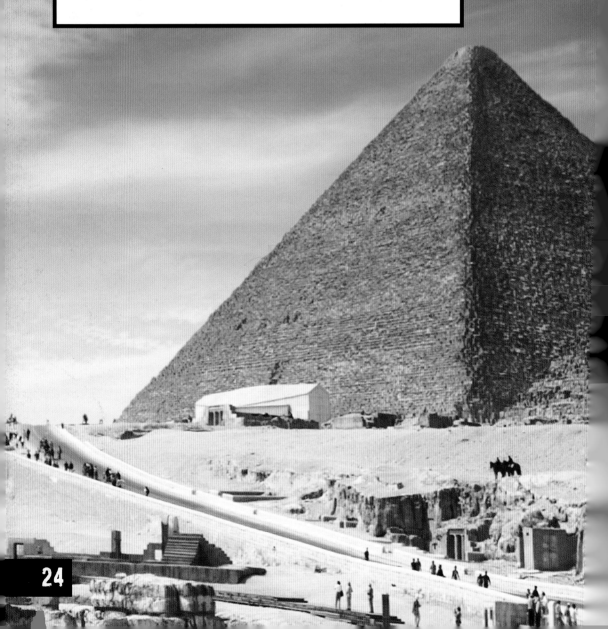

The pyramid is 138 metres high and covers an area of 5.3 hectares. It took 20 years to construct.

The pyramid was built to protect Pharaoh Khufu's body and his possessions. But, tomb robbers still found Khufu's burial chamber and stole its treasures.

Ivory statue of Khufu

BIG TOMBS

There are many huge tombs around the world.

The two-hectare burial ground of Qin Shi Huangdi, the First Emperor of China, contains the Terracotta Army.

The army consists of 8,000 life-like and life-sized statues of soldiers. It was believed that these soldiers would help the Emperor in the afterlife.

The Taj Mahal in India was built in 1631 by the Mughal Emperor Shah Jahan, for his wife who died during childbirth. It is 73 metres high.

The catacombs of Paris in France are underground tunnels and rooms. There are 300 kilometres of tunnels. The catacombs contain around six million bodies.

CONCLUSION

Now you've seen ten of the biggest things in the world.

What about the biggest thing in space?

In our galaxy, the biggest thing is the Sun. It is so big that you could fit one million Earths inside it.

The Sun is a burning ball of gas. It is 15.6 million degrees at its core. We can still feel its heat from 150 million kilometres away. Without it we would freeze to death!

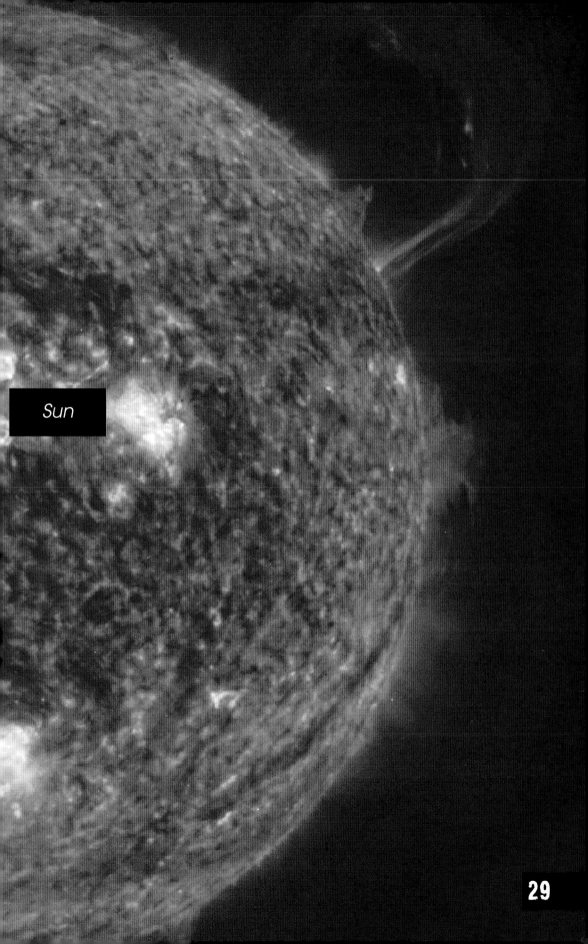

Sun

annual Something that occurs every year.

cargo Goods carried on a ship, aircraft or motor vehicle.

catacomb An underground cemetery consisting of tunnels and empty spaces for tombs.

commercially available Something that people can buy.

core The central part of something.

filter A porous device for removing impurities from a liquid that is passed through it.

krill Small shrimp-like marine creatures.

manufacture Making things, such as cars, on a large scale using machinery.

pollinate When an insect drops pollen inside a flower or plant, allowing it to produce seeds or fruit.

space shuttle A reusable spacecraft with wings that carries astronauts between Earth and a space station.

tomb A special building where the dead are buried.

vegetation Plants.

wingspan The measurement from the tip of one wing to the other.

BIG FACTS

- The largest butterfly is the Queen Alexandra's Birdwing. It has a wingspan of 28 centimetres and is the size of a pigeon.

- The land animal with the biggest mouth is the hippopotamus. It can open its jaws to nearly 180 degrees. The average adult male hippo can open its mouth 1.2 metres wide.

FIND OUT MORE ONLINE...

Bugatti
www.bugatti.com

CIA world fact book
www.cia.gov/library/publications/the-world-factbook/

Guinness World Records
www.guinnessworldrecords.com

National Geographic
www.nationalgeographic.com/

Tomato Fight
www.latomatina.org

INDEX